CW01512521

Original title:
Xylose Threads Below the Dragon Puff

Copyright © 2025 Swan Charm
All rights reserved.

Author: Sara Säde
ISBN HARDBACK: 978-1-80562-538-4
ISBN PAPERBACK: 978-1-80564-059-2

Myths in the Weave of the Night

In shadows deep where whispers dwell,
The moonlight casts its silken spell.
Creatures stir in twilight's grace,
With forgotten dreams, we share this space.

The stars above, like lanterns bright,
Guide wandering souls through endless flight.
Some tales are spun from ancient lore,
While others tread on unseen shore.

A phoenix rises from ashes gray,
In embered glow, it finds its way.
A unicorn roams through mist and dew,
As magic pulses, alive and true.

Beneath the veil, the fates entwine,
And every heartbeat sings divine.
With every breath, the legends speak,
Of truth in dreams, both strong and weak.

So gather 'round, ye hearts of light,
Embrace the myths that dance at night.
For in this realm, both fierce and bright,
We weave our tales, in shared delight.

Shards of Light in the Darkness

In shadows deep, a flicker bright,
A candle's glow, dispelling night.
Soft whispers weave through the air,
Guiding souls caught in despair.

Hope unfurls upon the breeze,
As light breaks through the twisted trees.
Each shard of dawn, a promise made,
Where darkness fades, and dreams invade.

From murky depths, a song begins,
With silver threads, where courage wins.
The night retreats to its dark lair,
As hearts embrace the warmth of care.

In every spark, a tale untold,
Of brave hearts light and spirits bold.
Together bound, we find our way,
Through shards of light, to brighter day.

Glimmers of an Awakened Heart

In stillness rests a beating drum,
Awakened, every breath becomes.
A gentle pulse, a tender rise,
Beneath the vast and open skies.

With every dawn, the heart reveals,
The hidden truths that time conceals.
In laughter's chime, and silence sweet,
Awakening dreams, where souls will meet.

Glimmers dance on thoughts anew,
Igniting warmth in morning dew.
With every step, a fresh start shines,
As love's embrace in stillness binds.

Through tangled paths and winding lanes,
We tread the joy, we shed the pains.
In every beat, a story grows,
In glimmers bright, the magic flows.

The Hidden Path of Serpentine Grace

In twilight's glow, a serpent glides,
Through whispering woods where shadow hides.
A winding path, both strange and fair,
Leads seekers deep, in secret air.

Each curve and twist, a gentle guide,
Through ancient tales where dreams abide.
The silent songs of leaves unfold,
Revealing truths, both shy and bold.

With grace it moves, a dancer's flair,
Through tangled roots and fragrant air.
It knows the spells of heart's embrace,
On hidden paths of serpentine grace.

With every turn, a spark of fate,
In labyrinthine dances, we await.
The wanderer knows the way is clear,
In quiet faith, the path draws near.

Embers of the Forgotten Forest

In shadows dense, where whispers sleep,
The forest holds its secrets deep.
Amidst the moss and ancient trees,
Lie embers stirred by gentle breeze.

Soft glimmers fade, yet linger still,
Each spark a memory to fulfill.
In twilight's grasp, the echoes roam,
A haunting tune that feels like home.

Old roots entwined in stories spun,
Of battles lost and victories won.
With every flicker, time reveals,
The depth of love, the pain that heals.

In silent nights where owls take flight,
The embers glow with eerie light.
They beckon forth the brave and bold,
To wander forth, their tales retold.

Spirals of Light in the Gloom

In shadows deep where whispers weave,
A gentle glow begins to cleave.
Spirals dance in twilight's grace,
Illuminating each hidden place.

Stars bleed silver on the night,
Casting dreams with tender light.
With every turn, the darkness fades,
Hope resides where fear cascades.

A symphony of colors bright,
Woven into the fabric of night.
Through the gloom, soft voices call,
Guiding hearts lest we should fall.

The winds of change begin to stir,
Carrying secrets, untouched by blur.
As spirals rise, shadows play,
Embracing dawn in a new day.

So dance with me 'neath the silken skies,
Where every dream begins to rise.
In spirals of light, we will bloom,
And cast aside all thoughts of gloom.

A Journey Through Phoenix Fire

From ashes cold, a spark ignites,
A fiery path, with boundless heights.
Through trials fierce, we learn to soar,
A journey carved through endless lore.

The flames that burn are soft yet bright,
They guide us home through darkest night.
With wings unfurled in crimson hue,
We rise above, our spirits true.

In every ember, stories dwell,
Of whispered dreams and spells we tell.
Through blazing trails of ancient lore,
We find our strength forevermore.

As phoenix cries break through the dark,
A chorus sings, igniting spark.
In every heart, a fire burns,
A sacred flame, the world it churns.

So heed the call, embrace the blaze,
In journey's fire, let courage raise.
Through trials met and battles fought,
In phoenix fire, our souls are caught.

The Enchanted Veil of Dusk

As day surrenders to the night,
An enchanted veil, a fleeting sight.
Soft shadows cling, a gentle embrace,
Whispers of magic in twilight's grace.

In dusky hues where secrets dwell,
A world awakes, its tale to tell.
With every star that graces the skies,
Mysteries bloom, like whispered sighs.

Beneath the veil, the fae take flight,
Dancing softly in silver light.
Their laughter echoes through the trees,
Carried gently by the evening breeze.

As twilight deepens, dreams align,
In this still hour, our spirits twine.
Time stretches thin in the quiet air,
Wrapped in wonder, free from care.

So let us linger, lost in the dusk,
Where magic thrives in the softening musk.
With open hearts, let shadows play,
In the enchantment of the fading day.

Revelations from a Blazing Heart

In the heartbeat of the night,
Fires ignite, casting their light.
With passion's flame, the truth will rise,
Revelations born from endless skies.

Each pulse a story, fierce and wild,
Echoes of dreams, unbeguiled.
With courage held against the dark,
A blazing heart ignites its spark.

Through trials faced, the shadows fade,
In every chance, a choice is made.
The heart reveals what eyes can't see,
In every breath, we find the key.

As embers glow, our spirits entwine,
In blazing truth, our fates align.
With every heartbeat, let love impart,
The strength we draw from a blazing heart.

So stand with me, let passions soar,
In revelations, we'll find the door.
Together we'll forge a path so bright,
With whispers born of love's pure light.

Weaving Dreams in the Mist

In the twilight's soft embrace,
A whisper of hopes takes flight,
With silver threads of starlit grace,
We weave our dreams through the night.

The fog wraps secrets in its shroud,
The forest breathes a gentle sigh,
With every heartbeat, soft and loud,
Our thoughts ascend, like birds on high.

In shadows deep, the visions bloom,
A tapestry of thoughts unseen,
Each flickering light dispels the gloom,
And paints the world, like magic, green.

As dawn breaks through the misty veil,
Our dreams awaken, take their flight,
And though we may stumble and fail,
The morning brings its warm sunlight.

We gather pieces of our past,
To stitch a canvas, bright and new,
With every moment, holding fast,
To dreams we weave and hope to pursue.

Secrets of the Shimmering Gloom

In the heart where shadows dance,
The secrets of night softly gleam,
Each flicker of fate, a whispered chance,
That spins the web of a complex dream.

Moonlit whispers call and beckon,
With every sigh, a story unfolds,
Amongst the murmur, a truth to reckon,
In shimmering gloom, the heart beholds.

Through the veil of the midnight sky,
Where glimmers of hope begin to show,
The spirits soar and the lost comply,
With echoes of laughter in the flow.

Each rustling leaf tells tales of yore,
Of sorrows borne and joys once found,
In the gloom's embrace, we seek for more,
Secrets entwined where dreams are bound.

As dawn tiptoes, the shadows fade,
With newfound light, the secrets gleam,
In the shimmer, a magic made,
From the whispers shared in the silken seam.

Threads of the Phoenix and the Serpent

From ashes born, the phoenix soars,
With flames ablaze and wings of gold,
In every rise, the spirit roars,
In a tale of courage untold.

Yet in the shadow, the serpent slinks,
With scales that glimmer, dark and bright,
Each thought it sows, like fleeting links,
Within the depths of the night.

Two destinies, entwined as one,
Through trials fierce, a lesson learned,
In every battle fought and won,
The fire of life forever burned.

The phoenix calls with a voice of light,
While the serpent holds a wisdom deep,
Together they dance, in cosmic flight,
In the hearts of those who dare to leap.

As dawn breaks forth, the world will see,
The bond of fate, a tapestry spun,
Of threads entwined, wild and free,
In the names of those who have just begun.

Echoes of the Ever-Shadowed Grove

In a grove where whispers echo clear,
The shadows weave their silent song,
With ancient stories held so near,
Where time has danced, and worlds belong.

Each tree stands tall, a guardian true,
With roots that cradle secrets vast,
In the still of night, they guide us through,
As echoes ring from ages past.

Beneath the stars, the spirits glide,
Through foliage dense, their laughter swells,
In every shadow, they reside,
Guardians of the tales they tell.

In moonlit glades, we find our way,
With courage stitched to every thought,
As echoes lead, we choose to stay,
Among the magic that time forgot.

So linger long in the grove's embrace,
For every whisper holds a key,
To unlock the heart of time and space,
And find the paths that set us free.

Enigmatic Bliss Beneath the Stars

In velvet night, the stars align,
Whispers of wonder, soft and divine.
A silver moon drapes all in grace,
As dreams awaken in this sacred space.

Luminous thoughts like fireflies glow,
Secrets of cosmos in twilight flow.
Each twinkle a tale, a story to tell,
In the heart of the night, where magic dwells.

With every sigh, the universe hums,
Echoes of love in the stillness come.
A dance of shadows beneath the light,
In enigmatic bliss, the world ignites.

Moments suspended in time's gentle hand,
Trust in the stars to guide as they stand.
Embrace the dreams that glimmer and gleam,
Beneath the stars, we weave our dream.

In quietude found in the vast unknown,
We seek the places we call our own.
Together in silence, where wishes take flight,
Enigmatic bliss beneath the night.

Patterns of a Firestorm Heart

In the depths of fire, a heartbeat glows,
Patterns of passion, where fervor flows.
Embers that twist like dancers in flight,
A symphony played in the cloak of night.

With every flicker, a story is spun,
The heat of the moment, a battle won.
Under the surface, a tempest roars,
Chasing the dreams that forever implore.

In shadows cast by the raging flame,
A lover's whispered, unspoken name.
Burning with longing, the flames entwine,
Patterns emerge like the stars that shine.

And in the ashes, new life will start,
From the remnants, rises a bold heart.
Each pulse a rhythm, each beat a song,
In the firestorm's dance, we all belong.

To feel the warmth that ignites our soul,
The beauty in chaos, the fiery whole.
Patterns discerned in a world aflame,
A journey where hearts learn to reclaim.

Dance of the Dragons in Twilight

In twilight's embrace, the dragons take flight,
Wings wide as shadows, a mesmerizing sight.
With scales that glimmer in hues of the dusk,
They swirl through the air, a sight so majestic.

They dance on the winds, in circles they glide,
Guardians of secrets, in whispers they bide.
Ancient and wise, with tales etched in fire,
They weave through the dreams, igniting desire.

With every heartbeat, a pulsing refrain,
The earth holds its breath, as they rise and wane.
In this fleeting moment, the world stands still,
Awash in the magic of twilight's thrill.

Legends unfold in the dusky glow,
Where spirits of old in the twilight sow.
A dance of the dragons, fierce and bright,
In the canvas of cosmos, they paint the night.

So carry the stories in hearts that ignite,
Whispered on breezes of magical night.
Let the dragons guide, with flames set to soar,
In the dance of the twilight, forevermore.

Flickering Voices of the Forest

In the heart of the woods, whispers unfold,
Flickering voices, both timid and bold.
Leaves rustle softly, the moonlight creeps,
Where nature's secrets in shadows meet.

Echoes of laughter, like streams in the air,
A symphony played in the cool, crisp flair.
The roots curl deeper, embracing the night,
As creatures awaken, in mystical flight.

With every step on the carpet of green,
The forest speaks softly, yet knows where we've been.
Hidden enchantments, await our gaze,
Flickering voices weave magical ways.

And through each branch, the stories take form,
A tapestry woven in nature's warm.
The call of the wild sings strong and free,
In the flickering voices, we find our spree.

So wander the paths where shadows unfold,
In the forest's embrace, let your spirit be bold.
For within the leaves and the sighs shared,
The flickering voices of magic declared.

Entwined by the Spirit of the Wild

In shadows deep where whispers play,
The spirits dance, both night and day.
A song of leaves, a call of the breeze,
Entwined in magic, hearts find ease.

Through tangled roots and ancient trees,
The wild reveals its secret keys.
With every step, the wisdom calls,
A journey begins where silence falls.

The moonlight paints the forest floor,
With every glance, we seek for more.
The spirit's touch, so soft, so bright,
Illuminates our paths with light.

In every rustle, in every sigh,
The wild's embrace lifts spirits high.
Together bound, through time and fate,
We find our kin, we resonate.

To nature's hymn, our souls unite,
In harmony, we take our flight.
Through wilds untamed, we roam as one,
Our hearts aflame, 'til day is done.

The Prismatic Walk of Destiny

Upon the path of shimmering hues,
A journey waits, with endless views.
Each step revealed, a story told,
The colors weave our fate in gold.

With every dawn, new shades appear,
Reflecting dreams and hopes held dear.
The choices made, like prisms bright,
Illuminate the darkest night.

Each fork inspires a twist in fate,
A dance with time, we hesitate.
But courage sprouts from seeds we sow,
On this prismatic walk, we grow.

Through vibrant fields and valleys wide,
Our hearts can soar, our fears subside.
For in this tapestry we thread,
The heart's true path shall never dread.

So take a breath and stride anew,
The colors glint; the world's askew.
Within each step, a tale will shine,
In destiny's embrace, we twine.

Woven Secrets from the Dreaming Realm

When twilight falls and stars are near,
The dreaming realm begins to clear.
Whispers linger in the night,
Woven secrets in soft light.

Beneath the veil of silent streams,
Our hopes entangle with our dreams.
In echoes deep, the futures call,
To leap with faith, we risk our all.

Each thread of thought, a silver line,
In moonlit visions, intertwine.
The journey through this mystic space,
A chance encounter, a sweet embrace.

The river flows with stories spun,
Of paths once taken, battles won.
In sleeping hours, we come alive,
In dreaming realms, our spirits thrive.

So close your eyes and drift away,
To find the secrets of the day.
With every dream, a world unfurls,
In woven whispers, magic swirls.

The Breath of Stars Beneath the Canopy

In ancient woods where shadows breathe,
The stars adorn the night's soft sheath.
A canopy of dreams above,
Whispers of the night, full of love.

Beneath the boughs, a silence thrums,
Where nature's heart in magic hums.
The world awakens in soft sighs,
As starlit dreams spread through the skies.

With every gust, the leaves will sway,
A lullaby from night to day.
Each shimmering spark within our gaze,
Reminds us of the endless ways.

To wander through this sacred space,
With every heartbeat, find our place.
For in the dark, the light reveals,
The breath of stars, our fate conceals.

So linger here, where wonders lie,
In breaths of stars that never die.
Embrace the night, let spirits soar,
Beneath the canopy, forevermore.

The Fabric of Silent Echoes

In shadows deep where whispers thread,
A tapestry of dreams lies spread.
Each echo stitched with silent care,
A world unseen, rich and rare.

The nightingale sings soft and low,
Beneath a veil of silver glow.
With threads of hope and heart entwined,
The fabric of the past we find.

Through corridors where phantoms play,
And memories drift like shades of gray.
In every stitch, a tale resides,
An artful weave where time abides.

These echoes call from distant lands,
Where time bends under gentle hands.
A realm where silence speaks in rhyme,
Forever echoes, lost in time.

So let us dance through shadowed halls,
Where the whispered past in stillness calls.
For in the fabric, secrets lie,
A tapestry of dreams must fly.

Whims of the Twilight Weaver

Under the cloak of twilight's grace,
The weaver spins at a gentle pace.
With threads of dusk and dreams anew,
She paints the sky in vibrant hue.

Each star a stitch, so bright, so bold,
In patterns spun of tales untold.
The moon, her guide, a lantern high,
Illuminates the night's soft sigh.

In every twirl, a wish is cast,
As day surrenders to the vast.
The winds they dance, the shadows weave,
In borrowed time, the heart believes.

The secrets spun in twilight's loom,
Unfold like petals, burst in bloom.
With every thread, a promise made,
In weavings rich, the night is laid.

So let the whims of twilight play,
As colors bleed and fade away.
For in this moment, magic swells,
As dreams arise and softly dwells.

Ensnared by Fantastical Delights

In glades where laughter dances free,
Fantastical delights call to thee.
A carousel of wonder spins,
Where every heart, a journey begins.

With sweet enchantments in the air,
With every glance, a secret shared.
The shimmering lights, a siren's song,
Inviting all to join along.

Through meadows bright with blooms of gold,
Adventure waits, both brave and bold.
In every shadow, a fable thrives,
Where magic lives and dreams survive.

Yet woven tight, the path may shift,
As thoughts entice, the spirits lift.
In fantastical realms where shadows creep,
Dreamers dance while others sleep.

So take a step, let wonder bloom,
Embrace the thrill, escape the gloom.
For in this realm, delight ignites,
And truths unfold in wondrous sights.

The Serpent's Silhouette in Starlight

Beneath the gaze of the midnight sun,
A serpent coils, its dance begun.
In starlit glades, it glides with grace,
A shadowed form in time and space.

Its scales reflect the light of dreams,
As whispered tales flow like gentle streams.
In every twist, a story spun,
Of battles fought and victories won.

The night it breathes, a mystic sigh,
As secrets cradle in the sky.
With every flick, the cosmos bends,
In twilight's hush, the magic mends.

A silhouette that twists and turns,
In starlit paths, through silence yearns.
With ancient wisdom, it glides along,
A melody of night's soft song.

So heed the call, embrace the night,
For in the dark, the serpent's flight.
In every shadow, wonders wait,
A starlit tale, a twist of fate.

Mysteries in the Dragon's Breath

In shadows deep where whispers fade,
A dragon's breath, a secret laid.
Through molten skies the echoes soar,
Ancient tales from days of yore.

With scales like night, it guards the sleep,
Of dreams and fears that secrets keep.
In ember glow, the truth ignites,
A flame that dances, sparks and flights.

The chirp of crickets, chorus sound,
A tale of magic, lost but found.
Beneath the stars, the night unfolds,
A symphony of myths retold.

In vaulted skies, the shimmer glows,
Where time stands still and magic flows.
Each breath a riddle, each sigh a spell,
In dragon's realm, all mysteries dwell.

So tread with care through veils of night,
For in the dark, there shines a light.
And with each step, in dreams we chase,
The dragon's breath, enchanted space.

Threads of the Arcane Forest

In twilight woods where shadows weave,
The trees hold secrets, tight they cleave.
Beneath the boughs, the whispers grow,
Of ancient magic, ebb and flow.

With every leaf, a story spins,
Of battle lost and timeless wins.
The roots entwined, like fates align,
In nature's grasp, the stars entwine.

The mossy floor, a carpet lush,
Where echoes of the past still hush.
A silver thread, a beckoning trail,
To realms of wonder, where dreams prevail.

In laughter pure, the brook does sing,
Of woodland sprites and fleeting spring.
Each step an ode, a dance of grace,
In the embrace of this sacred place.

So wander deep, let magic draw,
In arcane woods, the heart's pure law.
For every path, a tale unfolds,
In threads of time, the forest holds.

The Silken Riddle of Stars

In a velvet sky where wishes gleam,
The stars weave tales, a shimmering dream.
Each twinkle whispers, secrets shy,
A riddle spun, as days pass by.

With silken threads of moonlight spun,
They dance through night, till day is won.
In constellations, a map of fate,
Unfolding paths, that hearts create.

Like lanterns bright, they guide the way,
Through darkest woods, where shadows play.
A gentle nudge, a push from fears,
As dreams take wing, dissolved in tears.

The cosmos hums with magic's tune,
In every heart, a silver rune.
To seek the spark, that flickers true,
The silken riddle calls to you.

So gaze above, let visions swell,
In starlit night, where magic dwells.
With every breath, in wonder stay,
The riddle of stars will light your way.

Unraveling Scales of Aurora

In frosty realms, where colors blend,
The aurora's dance, a mystic friend.
With shimmering light, it weaves the air,
Unraveling secrets, everywhere.

Each scale that glimmers, tells a tale,
Of spirits bright that never fail.
Through valleys wide and mountains steep,
The whispers echo, a promise to keep.

The sky ablaze, a painter's dream,
In hues of gold and wisp of cream.
As night unfurls her velvet cloak,
The world beneath, in silence woke.

With every flicker, a heart can see,
The beauty bound in mystery.
So take a breath and look around,
In aurora's glow, true magic found.

The dance unravels, a story clear,
In dreams of light, we hold so dear.
With wonder ignited, and spirits high,
Unravel the scales, let your heart fly.

Luminous Fragments of Time

In the hush of twilight's song,
Luminous shards weaves through the throng,
Each moment a whisper of light,
A flicker that dances, taking flight.

With shadows that cradle the past,
Memories shimmer, so fragile and vast,
Threads of the universe spun tight,
In the embrace of the approaching night.

Stardust settles on dreams long lost,
A mirror reflecting the cost,
Every heartbeat a tale to unfold,
A rich tapestry, woven with gold.

Through the fabric of night we weave,
Holding the secrets of dreams we believe,
Time is a river, forever it flows,
Its luminous fragments, where magic grows.

In the quiet, the stillness is key,
To cherish the moments, to simply be,
Each glimmer a promise, a vow to keep,
In luminous fragments, our memories sleep.

Dreamcatchers in the Grove

Beneath the canopy, soft and green,
Dreamcatchers weave what has never been,
Catching whispers and laughter's sound,
In the heart of the grove, enchantment found.

The moonlight spills like silken threads,
Waking the wonder where magic spreads,
Stories linger in leaves so bright,
As shadows dance in the pale moonlight.

Each breeze carries a tale untold,
Of brave adventures, both shy and bold,
Dreamers gather, their eyes alight,
In the grove where dreams take flight.

Petals flutter like fleeting thoughts,
Whispers of wisdom, truths sought,
In each gentle rustle, a secret exchanged,
A bond, a moment, forever arranged.

So weave your dreams, let them ascend,
In the grove where wishes blend,
Catch the magic, let your heart roam,
For in this grove, you'll always feel home.

Flights of Fancy Through Woven Realms

Through velvet skies on wings we soar,
Flights of fancy to distant shores,
With every heart's whisper, we glide,
In woven realms where hopes abide.

Clouds like cotton, soft and sweet,
Carrying dreams to the rhythm of feet,
Bursts of color, a vibrant stream,
In this realm, we dance, we dream.

Stars are lanterns that shine so bright,
Guiding the lost through the endless night,
Each flicker a wish yet to be penned,
In flights of fancy, horizons extend.

Here, the impossible finds its place,
In a world where love and courage embrace,
Every heartbeat, a note of the song,
In woven realms where we all belong.

So take my hand, let's chase the dawn,
In this tapestry, we are reborn,
Through flights of fancy, we'll weave our dreams,
In the land of wonder where magic gleams.

Secrets of a Fiery Heart

In the hearth of dreams where embers glow,
Secrets whispered soft and low,
A fiery heart with passion ignites,
Illuminating the darkest nights.

Each pulse a story, waiting to rise,
With flames of courage that never dies,
In the dance of shadows, we find our part,
The truth ignited by a fiery heart.

Under the stars our souls entwine,
Unraveling threads of fate divine,
In the warmth of the fire, we see our spark,
With every heartbeat, a brave new mark.

So sing your song, let the echoes roam,
In the embrace of the fiery dome,
Secrets unveiled in glowing breath,
The heart's fierce flame conquering death.

For in every flicker, there lies a dream,
A promise to chase, a glittering beam,
In the depths of passion, where we restart,
We'll find our power in a fiery heart.

Chasing Shadows in Dragon's Breath

In the mist where whispers dwell,
Shadows dance and secrets swell.
Fires flicker, hearts ablaze,
Chasing dreams through smoky haze.

With each step, the echoes call,
Brave the night, lest darkness fall.
Dragon's breath warms the chill,
Spirits beckon, hearts can thrill.

Moonlight glints on emerald scales,
Guiding footsteps down hidden trails.
Stories woven through the night,
A quest for truth, a fiery flight.

In the heart of ancient trees,
Lies the magic carried in the breeze.
Chasing shadows, spirit strong,
In the dark, we all belong.

Threads Binding Us to the Unknown

In the tapestry of fate, we spin,
Each thread a story, each knot a sin.
Woven paths that intertwine,
Destinies dance with the divine.

Through the loom of time we tread,
Binding dreams with words unsaid.
With every twist, the future bends,
Hope and fear, where silence lends.

Shadows whisper secrets low,
In the fabric, truths will flow.
Threads of gold and silver gray,
Guide us gently on our way.

In unknown realms, brightly sewn,
The heart's true compass is our own.
Unraveling mysteries night and day,
In the threads that lead us astray.

Tales from the Glade of Mystique

In the glade where magic weaves,
Old trees speak of ancient leaves.
Whispers swirl in gentle sighs,
Secrets linger, never dies.

Creatures small, with eyes so bright,
Guardians of the fading light.
They tell tales of long-lost dreams,
In hushed voices, soft and sweet streams.

Rivers murmur, stones reply,
Echoes dance beneath the sky.
A world enchanted, safe and sound,
In shadows deep, the truth is found.

Beneath the moon, a promise glows,
In the glade where magic flows.
Tales of wonder, woven tight,
In a realm kissed by starlight.

Timeless Echoes of Ancestral Fire

Around the hearth, stories rise,
Flickering flames beneath the skies.
Ancestral fires lighting the way,
Carrying whispers of yesterday.

Embers pulse like heartbeats bold,
Tales of glory waiting to be told.
The warmth of legacy fills the air,
In every flicker, a silent prayer.

Eyes reflect the flame's soft glow,
In their depths, lost legends flow.
Gifted memories passed down the line,
Burning bright in hearts divine.

Through the years, Our spirits soar,
Echoes of wisdom, ancient lore.
In the light of the fire's embrace,
We remember our rightful place.

Enigmas Hidden in the Whispering Breeze

In twilight's hush, the secrets sigh,
A breeze so light, where shadows lie.
Whispers of tales, from ages past,
In hidden corners, long to last.

The trees converse, with leaves that dance,
Telling of magic, in night's expanse.
Mysteries woven in softest air,
Floating gently, without a care.

A flicker bright, a glimmer faint,
Hints of a world where dreams are quaint.
Footsteps linger, though none are seen,
In the world where the unseen's keen.

Listen closely, let your heart guide,
Through mazes of wonder, where dreams reside.
For in the breeze, the past unfolds,
The stories of wisdom, eternally told.

So find the path, let the winds steer,
To a realm where enchanted things appear.
In the whispering air, hold tight and see,
The enigmas waiting, just for thee.

Threads of the Forgotten

In moonlit rooms where dust motes play,
Threads of the past weave night into day.
Faded echoes of laughter resound,
In corners where memories are found.

Silk upon silk, bound gently tight,
Stories entwined in the fabric of night.
Each stitch a tale, each fold a sigh,
Of lives that lived, and dreams that die.

With needle and thread, the clock unwinds,
Unraveling visions that fate designed.
The forgotten glimmer, a spark of the soul,
Reviving the lost, making broken whole.

A tapestry rich, in colors vast,
Recalls the moments too quick to last.
Within the fibers, the heartbeats drum,
Of loved ones lost, and those yet to come.

So linger a while, on the edge of time,
Where threads intertwine, in rhythm and rhyme.
For in their embrace, the stories weave,
A legacy whispered, if we believe.

Remnants of the Hidden Flame

In the darkened grove, a flicker sways,
An ember glows, through misty haze.
The remnants dance, of flames long past,
Whispers of warmth that ever last.

Through ash and coal, the stories seep,
Of battles fought, and promises deep.
A flickering light, a call to keep,
In shadows where secrets carefully creep.

From woods untamed, the echoes flee,
Of fire's embrace, wild and free.
A pulse of heat where chill takes hold,
Gather the courage, be brave, be bold.

What once ignited the heart and mind,
In memory's hearth, the spark you'll find.
For remnants linger, though time may wane,
In each heart's chamber, the hidden flame.

So let it flicker, let it shine bright,
A beacon of hope in the cover of night.
In ashes of silence, let fire reclaim,
The warmth of love, the remnants of flame.

Pathways Cloaked in Serpent's Shadows

Through twisted paths where shadows creep,
The serpent winds, in silence deep.
Glimmers of light, so tempting, rare,
Yet concealed in darkness, danger dare.

With every turn, the whispers call,
Secrets entwined in the ancient hall.
Steps softly taken, the heartbeats race,
On pathways hidden, time won't erase.

Winding trails with a silken grace,
Guarded by serpents, a mystic place.
Every glance, a riddle's test,
To find the truths where shadows rest.

The dusk descends, with caution's hand,
Guide your spirit, make your stand.
For in the night, where fears may bloom,
The serpent's shadows can also loom.

So tread with care, awaken your sight,
For within the dark, lies the light.
Embrace the journey, let your heart flow,
On pathways cloaked, where mysteries grow.

Mystic Fabrics of a Forgotten Realm

In twilight's hush, where secrets weave,
Threads of magic dance, unseen but cleave.
Ancient whispers stir the quiet air,
Echoes of tales, a world laid bare.

On silken paths, lost spirits roam,
Carving their stories through night's dark dome.
With shimmering light the shadows play,
In the fabric of dreams, they gently sway.

Each stitch a promise, each knot a thread,
In a tapestry bright where the brave have tread.
The loom of fate spins tales of old,
Mysteries linger, waiting to unfold.

Beneath the stars, the weavers sigh,
Crafting fate where the night birds fly.
In colors bold, the past is told,
Through mystical patterns, brave and bold.

In the forgotten realm, we find our core,
A place where tales were birthed before.
So take a chance, let the fabric guide,
Through mystic realms where dreams abide.

Chasing Illusions in Dappled Air

In glimmers bright, the world is spun,
A fleeting glimpse, the chase begun.
Through dappled light and shadow's play,
We hunt the dreams that dance away.

With laughter soft, the winds do tease,
They lift our hopes upon the breeze.
Each shimmer beckons with a laugh,
A mirage fading, an endless path.

Yet brave we tread through magic's haze,
In every heart, a fiery blaze.
Like butterflies on sunbeams stray,
We seek the truth that leads astray.

With every turn, new visions gleam,
Illusions weave through just a dream.
Yet in our hearts, the spark remains,
A quest for light beyond life's chains.

So chase the visions, never wane,
For in the dance, there's little pain.
Through dappled air, we learn to fly,
In chasing dreams, we touch the sky.

Serpentine Whispers of the Night

In shadows deep, where silence lies,
The whispers curl, like lonesome sighs.
Serpents slither through veils of dark,
Tales of the lost, they gently spark.

Moonlight glints on scales of dark,
A secret path, an ancient arc.
With every hiss, the night unveils,
The stories hidden in mystery trails.

Softly they speak, in voices low,
Of midnight dreams, where lost souls go.
In breathless night, the shadows creep,
Guardians of secrets, profound and deep.

Beneath the stars, a tale unfolds,
Of magic whispered, of legends bold.
The serpentine lure calls us near,
To embrace the night without a fear.

In twilight's grasp, we find our way,
Chasing shadows that dance and sway.
With every whisper, we dare to seek,
The truths entwined in the silence bleak.

Veils of Breath and Ember

In embers bright, the dreams ignite,
Veils of breath float, soft as night.
Whispered secrets fill the air,
Letting our hearts a moment share.

Through glimmers warm, the worlds collide,
In every breath, there's magic inside.
The flicker, the glow, like fireflies,
Promises linger beneath the skies.

As shadows wrap their tender wings,
We find the solace that midnight brings.
With every ember laid to rest,
A whisper, a sigh — the soul's behest.

In veils of dusk, we softly tread,
Awakening echoes of things unsaid.
The breath of life, a rhythmic song,
Guides us gently, where we belong.

So breathe in deep, let embers spark,
Illuminate love in every dark.
In the sacred night where dreams take flight,
We'll dance with fire, hearts pure and bright.

Murmurs from the Heart of Nature

In the rustling leaves, secrets dance,
Whispers of the earth, a soft romance.
Through babbling brooks, a tale unfolds,
Of ancient woods where magic holds.

The daisies nod, in the warm sun's glow,
Nature's lullabies, in gentle flow.
With every breeze, a story spins,
Of weary travelers and their sins.

Beneath the boughs, shadows play,
In twilight's touch, where night meets day.
Each petal, a dream, so pure, so bright,
In the heart of nature, all feels right.

The stars peek down, a watchful eye,
Guardians of dreams that never die.
From mountain high to valley low,
Nature's embrace, a tender show.

So listen close, let silence reign,
Feel the warmth, embrace the pain.
For in the murmurs of this place,
Lies the essence of the human grace.

The Luster of Hidden Pathways

Follow the trail where shadows gleam,
In the quiet night, awaken a dream.
Twisting paths, with secrets to weave,
Each step taken, a heart to believe.

Through tangled thickets, the moonlight streams,
Casting silver on forgotten dreams.
With every whisper of the night air,
Longing hearts seek what's truly rare.

A glint of magic in an unseen door,
Tempting the brave to explore once more.
Hidden treasures, waiting to find,
The luster of paths to the open mind.

With every turn, a wonder appears,
Chasing the echoes of laughter and tears.
In hidden corners, where shadows play,
Secrets unfold, come what may.

So venture forth, with courage anew,
For the luster of pathways is meant for you.
Each journey holds what the heart seeks,
In the silent language, where nature speaks.

Celestial Hunting Grounds of the Mind

In the galaxy of thoughts, stars ignite,
Brilliant ideas, taking flight.
Every dream a shooting star,
Guiding the lost, showing where they are.

Through cosmic realms, imagination soars,
Unlocking the magic behind hidden doors.
Each notion twinkles, a bright spark,
Illuminating pathways through the dark.

In the vast expanse, where wonders abide,
Timid hearts grow bold, with nothing to hide.
Celestial whispers, calling you near,
Drawing you closer, dispelling the fear.

Hunting the visions that shimmer and glow,
Dancing through skies where wild dreams flow.
The universe speaks in a language profound,
In the silence of stars, wisdom is found.

So roam the galaxies, unconfined,
In the celestial hunting grounds of the mind.
For in that boundless space, you will see,
The magic of who you're destined to be.

Guardians of the Whispering Grove

In the heart of the grove, shadows play,
Nature's sentinels, old as the day.
With boughs that sigh and roots that hold,
They guard the stories, both timid and bold.

Ancient oaks stand, their wisdom deep,
Keeping secrets the forest will keep.
Each rustling leaf tells tales untold,
Of lovers, of battles, of treasures of gold.

The wildflowers bloom, painting the ground,
In colors of hope, where joy can be found.
With every gust, they dance and sway,
Guardians of dreams, leading the way.

As twilight falls, the creatures wake,
Murmurs of magic in every break.
From nightingale's song to owl's soft hoot,
In the whispering grove, nature's astute.

So trust in the guardians, watch and learn,
For in their embrace, the heart will yearn.
To wander the pathways of the ancient wood,
To find the magic where the spirit once stood.

Glimmers of Mythic Weavings

In forests deep where shadows play,
Whispers of old enchantments stay.
The trees, like guardians, hold the lore,
Of mythical heroes from days of yore.

With threads of silver and strands of gold,
Tales of the brave and the bold unfold.
In moonlit glades, their spirits dance,
Weaving the magic of fate and chance.

By starlit rivers, secrets flow,
Of lost kingdoms and the hearts they know.
A tapestry rich with colors bright,
Glimmers of dreams enfolded in night.

Through time's embrace, their songs still ring,
In every heartbeat, a longing to sing.
So listen close to the ancient call,
For in these weavings, you'll find it all.

Here the legends dwell, both fierce and kind,
A world of wonder, where souls unwind.
A journey woven in love and strife,
In the glimmers of mythic, eternal life.

Serenade of Celestial Dragons

Beneath the stars, they spread their wings,
The night sky hums with the magic it brings.
Celestial dragons, on currents glide,
In shimmering brilliance, they take to the tide.

With scales like sapphires, bright and rare,
They weave through constellations, light as air.
A serenade sung in a language so old,
Of wisdom and courage, a tale to be told.

They guard the realms where dreams unite,
With every breath, they ignite the night.
In their fierce embrace, all worries cease,
They cradle the cosmos, bestow peace.

Through clouds of stardust, their laughter rings,
Tales of adventure on ethereal wings.
Listen, dear heart, to their melodic thrill,
In the serenade sung, the universe stills.

These guardians of light, so mighty and grand,
Guide every traveler with a gentle hand.
In the vastness above, let your spirit soar,
With celestial dragons, forever explore.

The Loom of Enigmatic Night

In shadows cast by the silver moon,
The loom of night begins to croon.
With whispers spun through threads of grey,
The mysteries of dreams find their way.

Each star a stitch, each comet a thread,
Weaving tales of the living and dead.
In the tapestry of twilight's embrace,
The enigmatic dances through timeless space.

Beneath the veil of the silent sky,
Secrets awaken, and lost spirits fly.
The air fills with echoes of stories untold,
In the loom of night, their essence unfolds.

A soft lullaby sings to the heart,
Binding the world in its mystical art.
Through the depths of the dark, hope glimmers bright,
In the loom of enigmatic night.

So cradle your dreams in the hush of the hour,
For magic resides in the night's quiet power.
Together we wander, souls intertwined,
In the loom of the night, true wonders we find.

Beneath the Gossamer Veil

In gardens where the wildflowers play,
A veil of gossamer shades the day.
Whispers of magic fill the air,
As secrets unfold with tender care.

Dancing shadows beneath the trees,
Tell tales of love carried by the breeze.
With every flutter, enchantments grow,
In blossoms rich with a radiant glow.

Beneath the stars, the veil does sway,
Guarding the dreams that come out to play.
In moonlit moments, hearts entwine,
Lost in the magic that feels divine.

Through silver strands, the spirits glide,
In the tangled web where wishes abide.
With a gentle touch, they spin their tale,
In the soft embrace of the gossamer veil.

So close your eyes and breathe it in,
The essence of magic where dreams begin.
Under the veil, let your worries cease,
For in this realm, you'll find your peace.

Twilight's Dance of Ethereal Flames

In twilight's glow, the shadows play,
Whispers of night, where dreams decay.
Flames that flicker, dance and twirl,
In a world of magic, a soft unfurl.

Stars awaken, one by one,
Beneath the gaze of the silver sun.
Lost in the warmth of ember's embrace,
We find our haven in this mystic space.

The shadows stretch, entwined with light,
Crimson hues in the velvet night.
Echoes of laughter, sweet and rare,
On twilight's breath, they linger in air.

A whispered promise, the night will keep,
In fire's glow, we're not asleep.
Ethereal flames, a guiding guide,
Through dreams we dance, where secrets hide.

In twilight's realm, we hold the key,
Unlocking paths to what will be.
With every flicker, a story told,
In the heart of night, our lives unfold.

The Loom of Forgotten Fables

In hidden corners, tales are spun,
Threads of ancient lore begun.
Whispers linger in the woven seams,
A tapestry of lost, sweet dreams.

The loom awaits, with patience fine,
Weaving moments, a life divine.
Each stitch a memory, a tale to tell,
In the fabric of time, we weave so well.

Ghostly figures dance and twine,
Through silken paths, where shadows shine.
Fables forgotten, yet still they breathe,
In the looms of memory, we believe.

Echoes of laughter, whispers of woe,
In this haunted place, our spirits flow.
With every turn of the spinning wheel,
The heart of the story, we begin to feel.

In threads of gold and silver bright,
We cast our hopes into the night.
For every story is a bridge, a way,
To keep the past alive, come what may.

Shimmering Paths Through Mystic Woods

In the heart of woods where shadows meet,
Shimmering paths beneath our feet.
We wander where the wild things sing,
In secret glades, where fairies cling.

Sunbeams filter through emerald leaves,
In this enchanted realm, the heart believes.
Laughter dances on the breeze,
As nature whispers with gentle ease.

Mossy carpets cradle our steps,
As ancient trees guard their secrets and depth.
The air is thick with fragrant blooms,
In this embrace, our spirit blooms.

Clouds of dreams drift on the air,
Every whisper tells us to dare.
To follow the shimmer, the paths that glow,
In the mystic woods, we let love flow.

With each turn, a story unfolds,
Of battles fought and glories untold.
Within these woods, magic thrives,
In shimmering paths, our souls arrive.

Crackling Breaths of the Green Abyss

In the green abyss, where shadows creep,
Life awakens from its slumber deep.
Crackling breaths in the damp night air,
Whispers of secrets, beyond compare.

Ancient roots intertwine and twist,
In a world of wonder, we can't resist.
The glow of fireflies glimmers bright,
Guiding us through the mystical night.

A symphony plays, of rustling leaves,
In this sacred space, the heart believes.
Echoes of magic in every sound,
In the green abyss, our spirits are found.

Beneath the canopies, mysteries brew,
In the shadows, dreams come true.
With crackling breaths, nature sings,
Of life renewed and wondrous things.

Through tangled vines, our journeys wind,
In every corner, enchantments bind.
In this verdant world, we come alive,
In the green abyss, we learn to thrive.

Shadows of the Daring Serpent

In twilight's grasp, the serpent winds,
With scales that shimmer, secrets find.
Through tangled woods, it weaves its tale,
In whispered breaths, elusive, pale.

Its eyes like embers, blazing bright,
A creature born of darkest night.
With daring heart and cunning grace,
It dances through the moonlit space.

Beneath the boughs of ancient trees,
Where shadows murmur with the breeze.
A guardian of the hidden paths,
In every twist, the magic lathes.

With every movement, tales unfold,
Of daring deeds and treasures bold.
The serpent glides, a fleeting glance,
In realms where only few would chance.

So heed the call when darkness stirs,
The daring serpent softly purrs.
A promise wrapped in mystic dreams,
To guide the brave, or so it seems.

Tapestry of Forgotten Dreams

In cobwebbed corners, memories hide,
A tapestry of dreams, cast aside.
Threads of silver, woven tight,
In the tapestry's embrace, take flight.

Faded whispers in the night,
Echoes of fervor, out of sight.
A gentle tug of hopes once bright,
Rekindled now, they seek the light.

Each pattern speaks of paths once crossed,
Of laughter gained and love embossed.
Yet woven through the strands of time,
Are tales of sorrow, silence, rhyme.

With every stitch, a story swells,
Of longing hearts, forgotten spells.
In dreams once lost, now brought to bear,
The tapestry unfolds with care.

So let us thread our wishes true,
In colors bold, in shades anew.
For in the weaving of our schemes,
We find the power of forgotten dreams.

The Dance of Radiant Spires

Among the clouds, the spires rise,
With gleaming crowns that kiss the skies.
Each point a wish, a hope, a fire,
In harmony, they dance, aspire.

The golden sun ignites their gleam,
Reflecting light in every beam.
A symphony of stone and light,
That twirls and sways through day and night.

In twilight's glow, they gently sway,
A ballet in the fading day.
With whispers soft as evening falls,
They answer to the night's soft calls.

From peak to peak, the shadows chase,
In this ethereal, sacred space.
A waltz of dreams, both bold and bright,
That weaves the world with pure delight.

So gaze above where spires gleam,
Embrace the magic, the grand scheme.
In their dance, our spirits rise,
Forever anchored in the skies.

Lurking in the Verdant Abyss

In depths where leafy secrets dwell,
The verdant abyss casts its spell.
Among the ferns, where shadows creep,
A world of wonders, lost in sleep.

With every rustle, whispers call,
The ancient trees stand proud and tall.
A childhood's curse or dreamer's quest,
In tangled roots, the heart finds rest.

Creatures spiral in the gloom,
With eyes that glint, they weave the doom.
Yet in this dark, a beauty gleams,
The wild, untamed, where magic teems.

Through emerald paths, the silence grows,
In hidden corners, nature flows.
From every breath, a tale begun,
Of darkened nights and playful sun.

So wander forth, embrace the wild,
Let wonder guide the heart of child.
In verdant depths, both dark and sweet,
Awaits the truth, the bittersweet.

The Allure of Shimmering Dreams

In twilight whispers, shadows play,
A canvas spun in hues of gray.
Each fleeting thought, a glimmer bright,
We chase the echoes of the night.

With silver stars like fireflies,
They hold the magic of our sighs.
In dreams we weave, with silken thread,
The tales of all we've wished and said.

Soft lullabies in starlit streams,
Awaken vessels full of dreams.
Imagination takes its flight,
A tapestry of pure delight.

From depths of heart, our yearnings rise,
In shimmering depths of endless skies.
A spark of hope, a wish concealed,
In fantasy, our fates revealed.

So gather 'round, let spirits gleam,
And draw from worlds that dare to dream.
In every heartbeat, let us find,
The lovely lull of magic's kind.

The Dance of Light in the Abyss

In shadows deep, where echoes dwell,
A dance begins, an ancient spell.
With whispers soft, the darkness sways,
And beckons forth the light's embrace.

Fleeting glimmers pierce the night,
A tempest turning dark to light.
In cosmic waltz, the stars ignite,
And shimmer bright, a wondrous sight.

Lost souls tread the path of fate,
Embraced by shimmering hands of late.
In quiet corners, secrets spin,
Awakening what lies within.

With every twirl, the void does sing,
Of hope reborn, of love's soft wing.
Beneath the strains of twilight's grace,
The dance reveals a sacred space.

So let us sway, 'neath cosmic skies,
In every heartbeat, spirit flies.
For even in the deepest night,
The dance of light will guide us right.

Spirits Twined in Celestial Silk

In golden threads of moonlit haze,
Ethereal forms in gentle praise.
With whispered breaths, in twilight's grace,
We weave our dreams in sweet embrace.

Each spirit glows, a radiant fire,
Vows of love that never tire.
In starlit realms where shadows blend,
We share our hearts, our souls extend.

With silken ties that softly bind,
We journey forth, our fates aligned.
In unity, our voices rise,
A symphony that spans the skies.

Through veils of time, we wander far,
Each twinkling fate, a guiding star.
In cosmic dance, our spirits sing,
The joy and peace that love can bring.

So hand in hand, let hope ignite,
In treasured bonds of purest light.
For in this dance, we truly find,
The legacy of heart entwined.

Costa of the Celestial Wyrm

Upon the shore of dreams untold,
Where legends breathe and fate unfolds.
The celestial wyrm, in splendor bright,
Guarding secrets 'neath the night.

With scales that shimmer like the sea,
It whispers tales of what shall be.
In arcane waves of time and space,
We seek the wisdom of its grace.

As currents swirl and tides align,
We dive into the world divine.
In every crest, the wyrm's embrace,
We find our place, we find our pace.

With every breath, the ocean sighs,
A lullaby 'neath endless skies.
In the flow of stars and dreams untamed,
The wyrm holds power, yet unclaimed.

So let us sail on waves of lore,
To realms of light, forevermore.
In harmony with wyrm and wave,
We seek the paths our hearts can brave.

Whispers of Celestial Weaves

In twilight's glow, the stars align,
They spin the tales of fate divine.
With gentle hands, the moonlight weaves,
A tapestry that never leaves.

From depths of night, soft secrets sigh,
As constellations softly fly.
Each twinkle holds a whispered word,
In harmonies of light, unheard.

The comets blaze with fiery grace,
While galaxies embrace their space.
The wind carries old legend's breath,
In cosmic tales, both life and death.

Beyond the clouds, where dreams take flight,
In realms of wonder, pure delight.
The universe in stillness glows,
A boundless world where magic flows.

So close your eyes, let stardust fall,
As night unveils its ancient call.
With every pulse, the heavens share,
The whispers of the cosmic air.

Shadows of Serpent Dreams

In twilight's hush, the shadows creep,
Where ancient serpents stir from sleep.
Their scales reflect the moon's pale gleam,
In whispers soft, they weave a dream.

The forest echoes with their glide,
As secrets in the dark abide.
Each rustle tells of ages past,
Their tales entwined, forever cast.

Through tangled roots and silvered streams,
They slumber deep in woven dreams.
The night enfolds, caressing slow,
Where mystic paths of moonlight flow.

The twilight veil, a cloak of mist,
Hides visions that the stars have kissed.
In shadows, truth and myth are spun,
A dance of dusk till night is done.

So tread with care on whispered ground,
For here, the lost and found are bound.
In serpent's dream, your heart may find,
The mysteries of the dark entwined.

Tapestry of the Ancient Sky

Beneath the arch of endless night,
The ancients weave their tales of light.
With stars like threads, they stitch and tie,
A tapestry within the sky.

Galaxies swirl in rhythmic grace,
While history finds its rightful place.
Together spun, both bold and bright,
The stories lost, reclaimed by night.

In every gleam, a saga's birth,
The dance of time, the cradle of earth.
Each constellation holds a key,
To secrets locked in memory.

The moon, a sentinel of dreams,
Reflects the sun's soft golden beams.
In shadows cast, the eras blend,
In cosmic tales that never end.

So gaze upon that celestial weave,
And in its beauty, dare believe.
For in the night, we find our way,
In woven stars that brightly sway.

Echoes from the Verdant Abyss

In verdant depths where silence reigns,
The echoes stretch like whispered chains.
Among the roots, where memories grow,
The heart of nature beats down low.

The leaves converse in rustling sighs,
As ancient wisdom softly flies.
In shadows deep, where spirits tread,
Their stories rise from earth and bed.

The gnarled trees with arms outspread,
Hold tales of life and dreams long dead.
Each breath a song, both sweet and wild,
In nature's cradle, pure and mild.

Through the moss, the whispers thread,
In patterns soft, where souls have fled.
The forest hums its sacred tune,
In symphony with sun and moon.

So wander slow, let silence speak,
In verdant realms, both rich and bleak.
For in these echoes, truths abide,
In nature's arms, our hearts confide.

Threads of Enchantment in Twilight

In twilight's glow, the whispers start,
Threads of magic weave the heart.
Stars awaken, glimmering bright,
Spinning dreams into the night.

A breeze that dances, soft and low,
Guides the way where shadows go.
Each step taken, mysteries call,
In the twilight, we find it all.

The hidden paths where fairies tread,
Through the fabric, softly spread.
Nature's pulse, a lullaby,
Tells the tales of days gone by.

With every stitch, a story flows,
Threads of wonder gently grows.
As night unfurls her velvet cloak,
In whispered dreams, our spirits soak.

So let us gather, hearts entwined,
In twilight's breath, our fates aligned.
For in the dusk, enchantments weave,
A tapestry we dare believe.

Lurking Fire Beneath the Canopy

Beneath the trees, where secrets breathe,
Lurking flames of magic seethe.
A flicker here, a spark of light,
In shadows deep, they dance from sight.

The forest whispers tales of old,
Of ancient hearts and treasures bold.
Among the roots, in earth and gloom,
The lingering embers find their room.

A crackling hush, the night ignites,
With fiery tales and starry flights.
In every rustle, in every sigh,
The canopy holds time gone by.

Threads of warmth in chill's embrace,
A magic spark in nature's grace.
As moonlight glimmers through the leaves,
The heart of fire, the forest weaves.

So wander deep through woodland shade,
Where here inside, the light won't fade.
For in the dark, where spirits play,
Lurking fire shall light the way.

Secrets Woven in Moonlight

Under the moon's soft, silver glow,
Secrets dance, a timeless flow.
Every shadow, every sigh,
Whispers tales that never die.

In the stillness, mysteries sing,
Of hidden realms and ancient things.
Starlit patterns in cool night air,
Weaving magic, rich and rare.

The silken threads of dreams entwined,
In moonlit paths, our fates aligned.
Gentle beams on hidden glades,
Where twilight's touch in silence fades.

As fireflies weave their light and dash,
Secrets shimmer, fade, and flash.
In every crevice, in every beam,
A world alive, a waking dream.

So let us wander, hand in hand,
Through moonlit spells, a mystical land.
For in the dark, where hopes ignite,
The secrets woven pure and bright.

The Sylvan Echo of Time

In forests deep, where echoes sigh,
The sylvan whispers softly cry.
Time flows like rivers, deep and wide,
In each embrace, the past confides.

Beneath the boughs, where shadows play,
The memories linger, night and day.
Every rustling leaf, a story shared,
Of battles fought and dreams declared.

A heart of wood, a soul of stone,
In nature's grasp, we are not alone.
The eons pass, yet still we find,
In sylvan echoes, we're intertwined.

Through timeless paths, we wander free,
With every step, we hear the plea.
Of ancient trees that stand so tall,
Guardians watching over all.

So listen close as night descends,
For in the stillness, magic bends.
The sylvan echo of time's embrace,
A timeless dance, a sacred space.

Fantasies Whispered in the Winds

In the hush of a twilight breeze,
Whispers of dreams dance with ease.
Stars blink softly, secrets unfold,
Untold tales of the brave and bold.

Through the meadows where shadows play,
Magic lingers, come what may.
A flicker of hope in a faded sigh,
Adventures beckon, oh, soaring high.

From golden fields to skies of blue,
Fantasies weave, both old and new.
Each leaf a story, each gust a song,
In this realm, where we all belong.

With moonlit paths that gently gleam,
We wander where nothing's as it seems.
For in the winds, magic is sown,
A tapestry of dreams fully grown.

So let the winds carry your heart,
Embrace the magic, take your part.
For in the whispers, treasures await,
Awake the dreamer—it's never too late.

Threnody of the Wandering Hearth

The embers flicker, stories unfold,
A wandering hearth with warmth untold.
Where echoes of laughter fill the night,
And shadows waltz in the flickering light.

Once it burned bright in love's embrace,
Now it wanders, seeking its place.
Through fields of sorrow, across the seas,
A threnody carried by the whispering breeze.

In every corner where silence reigns,
The hearth remembers, it knows the pains.
Of homesick travelers, lost and worn,
Each flame a beacon, each spark reborn.

The lullaby of lost dreams calls,
Through darkened halls and ancient walls.
It sings of comfort, of ceaseless quests,
Of hearths untraveled and uninvited guests.

Yet hope still dances in the glow,
As echoes of love begin to flow.
With every ember, a promise shines,
As wandering hearts seek what intertwines.

Flickerings of a Shattered Dream

In the mirage of moonlit schemes,
Flickers glimmer of shattered dreams.
Once a treasure, now a sigh,
Whispered regrets as time drifts by.

Through tattered pages of yesterday,
Faded echoes find their way.
Each shard a memory, bright and dim,
A song of loss, a sorrowful hymn.

Yet through the cracks, new light may creep,
From broken dreams, treasures keep.
For every shadow that seeks to hide,
A flicker of hope will abide.

Thus hearts entwined in quiet despair,
Seek meaning within the thin air.
For what is broken can still repair,
In the dance of dreams, we still dare.

So gather the fragments, piece them near,
Crafting a story from what we fear.
In the flickerings, let our spirits soar,
Shattered dreams can inspire much more.

A Chorus of Fire and Earth

In the heart of tempest and calm,
A chorus resounds, a soothing balm.
Flames intertwine with the roots below,
A dance of elements, a vibrant glow.

From ashes and earth, life begins,
A symphony where the soul spins.
Each note a whisper, each chord a scream,
Together weaving a timeless dream.

Winds carry tales of struggles fought,
Through trials faced and lessons taught.
Fire and earth, in balance they weave,
A tapestry of hope, a chance to believe.

As mountains rumble and rivers flow,
The chorus rises, with strength to sow.
In every heartbeat, in every breath,
Life's vibrant music, defying death.

So let the harmony find its place,
In every corner of time and space.
For we are the echoes, we are the flames,
A chorus of fire, earth, and dreams.

Rivers of Light through the Gnarled Woods

Through twisted boughs the whispers weave,
A glow that dances, one might believe.
Reflections shimmer on the darkened stream,
In this enchanted realm, all is a dream.

The ancient oaks, they gently sway,
Guardians of stories lost in the fray.
With each soft rustle, a tale is spun,
Of light and shadow, of moon and sun.

The river sings with a silvered tongue,
Of ages past where the hearts were young.
In waters deep, the secrets flow,
A journey that only the brave may know.

Mysteries float in the night's embrace,
Silhouettes dance, a ghostly trace.
The fireflies twinkle, a fleeting sight,
Guiding the lost in the hush of night.

In gnarled woods where wonders unfold,
Every shadow speaks, every story told.
We wander through dreams, hand in hand,
Finding solace in this sacred land.

Shadowed Visions of the Hearth

In the gloaming where warm embers glow,
Stories arise from the ashes below.
A flickering dance of tales untold,
Whispers of warmth in the winter's cold.

The shadows gather, their secrets to share,
Soft murmurs of love hang thick in the air.
Hearths crackle softly, a lullaby sweet,
Binding our hearts in the night's gentle heat.

Through the pane, the world drifts away,
Outside in the darkness, the children play.
But here in this light, we're evermore near,
Echoes of laughter, drawing us near.

As stories unwind like the threads of a cloak,
Each whispered word a delicate stroke.
In the glow of the fire, we find our own fate,
Carved in the wood, for it's never too late.

Shadowed visions of what has been lost,
We gather our dreams, despite any cost.
To the hearth we return, with spirits alight,
In the solace of home, we conquer the night.

Ancestral Echoes Through the Ages

In the dust of the past, we find our way,
Echoes of ancestors softly sway.
Their whispers linger like the morning dew,
Guiding our journeys as we seek what's true.

Through time-worn paths, our spirits roam,
Carried on currents that call us home.
With every step, we honor the lost,
Their stories steeped in the life we exhaust.

The roots of our being stretch deep and wide,
Tales woven through the heart, where they bide.
In the twilight hours, we feel their embrace,
A warm reminder of love's gentle grace.

Ancestral faces in the flicker of light,
Guide us through darkness, turning wrongs to right.
Each memory echoes, a bridge to the past,
In the dance of the ages, forever cast.

As boundless time flows like an endless sea,
Our heritage lives in the heart's tender plea.
To the whispers of time, we silently sway,
In the fabric of kinship, forever we stay.

The Spark of Distant Fireflies

In a meadow aglow with dreams untold,
Fireflies twinkle like jewels of gold.
A spark in the night, a chance to ignite,
Whispers of magic, veiled just out of sight.

They flicker and dance, a celestial guide,
Drawing us close to the fate that resides.
Children of light in the moon's gentle beam,
In the stillness of night, they weave a new dream.

As we chase their glow, a giggle escapes,
Adventure awaits where the wild heart shapes.
In laughter and wonder, our spirits unite,
Together we wander, enchanted by night.

The spark of a moment, so tender, so bright,
Moments of magic splash colors of light.
In this vast universe, a flicker we chase,
Where fireflies guide us to love's warm embrace.

So let your heart carry the light ever true,
For in each little spark, there's a world to pursue.
With the dance of the fireflies lighting the way,
Embrace all the magic the night holds at bay.

The Flicker of Resilient Spirits

In shadows deep, the courage grows,
A spark ignites where hope still glows.
Through trials faced, the hearts unite,
To rise again, to seek the light.

Each whispered tale of battles fought,
In quiet strength, their wisdom taught.
For echoes of the past remind,
The resilient spirit, fiercely kind.

Though storms may rage and winds may howl,
The flicker shines, the heart's own prowl.
With every setback, seeds are sown,
For from the grit, true strength is grown.

In realms of dusk, when fears arise,
The ember glints in hopeful eyes.
With every breath, a chance to live,
The will to fight, our gift to give.

Together bound, we weave our fates,
In unity, the heart elates.
For through the dark, we forge our way,
In flickering light, we find our stay.

Patterns of the Celestial Dragon

In twilight skies, the dragon flies,
A tapestry of stars that rise.
With scales of gold and wings of grace,
It dances through the starlit space.

Each constellation tells a tale,
Of ancient forces that prevail.
In swirling mists, its secrets weave,
A cosmic dance, we dare believe.

As lunar beams embrace the night,
The dragon glows, a radiant sight.
With fiery breath, it lights the way,
Igniting dreams that softly sway.

In whispers soft, it calls the brave,
To soar with it, beyond the grave.
For in the sky, our fates align,
In patterns drawn by hands divine.

A guardian of the boundless skies,
With knowing gaze and ancient sighs.
It teaches us to find our song,
In harmony, where we belong.

So let us rise on wings of hope,
Emboldened by the starlit scope.
With every beat, we join its flight,
In patterns spun by endless light.

Breathing Life into Forgotten Myths

In ancient woods where shadows dwell,
The whispered tales begin to swell.
Forgotten myths, now stirred to breathe,
Awakening dreams from time's own sheath.

With every rustle, nature sings,
Of creatures born with mystic wings.
The echo of their laughter calls,
For magic lingers in these halls.

In moonlit glades, the spirits roam,
Each tale a thread that leads us home.
To realms where giants walked in pride,
And wisdom flowed like a gentle tide.

With courage found in timeless lore,
We seek the paths that were before.
To breathe new life into the past,
To hold the moments, ever vast.

The heart remembers what time forgets,
In every story, the magic begets.
Through whispers soft, and shadows' glow,
The myths return, as rivers flow.

So gather close, let feelings rise,
As legends dance through starlit skies.
For in their breath, we come alive,
In forgotten myths, we truly thrive.

Flickers of Twilight Upon the Hearth

In twilight's glow, the embers spark,
Casting warmth in shadows stark.
With every flicker, stories weave,
As time stands still, we dare believe.

Upon the hearth, the memories glow,
Of laughter shared, long years ago.
The whispers of the past remain,
In flickers danced, in joy and pain.

A gathering where spirits meet,
The heart's own rhythm, soft and sweet.
With candles lit and hopes held tight,
We find our solace in the night.

Through tales retold, the fire sings,
Of love and loss, of fleeting things.
In twilight's grasp, we find our place,
In every glance, a warm embrace.

As shadows stretch and twilight deepens,
The heart ignites, its warmth it deepens.
Together bound in this sacred space,
Flickers of joy, in time's embrace.

So let us gather, night so clear,
With every ember, we draw near.
For in this warmth, we live and thrive,
In flickers of twilight, we come alive.

Whispers of Celestial Fibers

In twilight's gentle, silver glow,
Stars weave tales that softly flow.
Each twinkle holds a secret bright,
A whisper soft as velvet night.

On woven threads of dreams and lore,
Celestial fibers softly soar.
Across the sky, they twist and turn,
Illuminating hearts that yearn.

Bright comets dance, with grace untamed,
Through starry paths, their stories claimed.
The cosmos hums a lullaby,
Of distant worlds that soar on high.

Within the silence, secrets bloom,
In cosmic gardens, free from gloom.
Each glowing orb, a guide divine,
A beacon through the vast design.

So let your dreams, like starlight, spark,
Woven in the evening dark.
For every wish, a dream's embrace,
Whispers echo in time and space.

Secrets Woven in Moonlight

By silver threads of moonlit grace,
The night reveals its secret face.
With every beam, a story spun,
Of battles lost and victories won.

In shadows deep, where dreams reside,
The whispers of the past abide.
Each sigh the breeze begins to weave,
A tapestry we dare believe.

The stars conspire to light the way,
While nightingale tunes softly play.
In twilight's hush, our secrets sigh,
To dance beneath the velvet sky.

The silver moon, a watchful eye,
Over wishes that dare to fly.
With every pulse, a fate entwined,
In moonlit realms, our hearts aligned.

The night reveals the truth within,
Of dreams forgotten, hopes akin.
With every shadow, secrets bloom,
In ethereal threads, life finds room.

Beneath the Emerald Canopy

In emerald groves where whispers dwell,
The forest speaks, a magic spell.
With every rustle in the leaves,
A tale of wonders, nature weaves.

The sunlight filters, dappled light,
Painting dreams in hues so bright.
Beneath the boughs, the spirits play,
In laughter soft, they fade away.

With every breeze, a dance ensues,
In ancient songs, the heart imbues.
The tales of yore, the trees confide,
In gentle murmurs, love and pride.

Through tangled roots, the echoes flow,
Of life and magic, ebb and glow.
In every shadow, wisdom hides,
Beneath the wings where nature glides.

So wander deep, where shadows gleam,
And lose yourself in nature's dream.
For in the woods, a world unfolds,
With every step, a tale retold.

Echoes of the Enchanted Loom

In twilight's hush, the looms awake,
With threads of gold, their stories make.
An ancient dance of fate and time,
Woven dreams in rhythm and rhyme.

With every pull, a whispered sigh,
Of hearts entwined and hopes that fly.
The fabric hums a haunting tune,
Underneath the watchful moon.

The weaver spins a tale so rare,
Of heroes brave, and love laid bare.
With colors bright as dawn's embrace,
Each woven thread, a timeless grace.

As shadows play, the patterns twine,
In every stitch, the stars align.
A tapestry of dreams unspooled,
In enchanted threads, life is ruled.

So let the echoes guide your way,
In woven worlds where wishes sway.
For in the loom of fate and chance,
Life's magic weaves a timeless dance.